NICOLE

JOHNNIE: FOR OPENING STATEMENT —
HOW NICOLE ABUSED ME!

- Hair in sink
- Lipstick smootches on nice towels
- Wore annoying jangly bracelets
- Said I snored — NO EVIDENCE!
- Whiny "hit me" voice
- Left bit of juice in container so she didn't have to go buy new one
- Played Neil Diamond ALL THE TIME!
- Didn't "get" football
- **SHOP SHOP SHOP**

I SWEAR TO TELL THE TRUTH, THE WHOLE TRUTH, AND NOTHING BUT THE TRUTH, SO HELP ME RHONDA — HELP ME GET HER OUT OF MY HEART.

NOTE: Ask F. Lee Bailey what "F" stands for.

JOHNNIE C. — POSSIB. ANGLE: DNA test like SAT test — UNFAIR TO BLACKS!

OBJECT!
OBJECT!
OBJECT!

<u>NOTE!!</u> <u>GET RELIGION!!!!</u>

<u>BORN AGAIN</u> — HAVE TO READ BIBLE

(THICK BOOK - AUDIO VERSION ?

ASK ROSEY GRIER)

<u>MUSLIM</u> — O.X. SIMPSON - EL?

<u>BUDDHIST</u> — DUMB-LOOKING DUDS, TOFU BURGERS (YECHH!)

NINJA TURTLES?

<u>MORMON</u> — NO BOOZE, NO COFFEE, NO SMOKING, NO NOTHING.

PROBABLY NO "NEGROES" EITHER.

<u>JEWISH</u> — COULD BE SMART MOVE - INSIDE TRACK WITH

H-WOOD STUDIO EXECS, AGENTS, ETC. (ASK BOB. SHAP.-

HAVE TO WEAR DOILY ON HEAD? GET DICK CLIPPED?) SHORTER BIBLE?

Nice Things I've Done

THE MAN

O.J.

① Put money in those little cans by the cash register

② Big tipper

③ Wave to people and smile — A <u>**LOT**</u>

④ Signed autographs for free (time to rethink this policy?)

⑤ Voted best something or other in 1990 (1990?) by do-good

group in Phoenix. Jaycees?

⑥ <u>Really</u> into recycling.

WHY I'M NOT CAPABLE OF MURDER

- Not wacko "killer type" with scary tattoos
- Cry in movies
- Life of party - clown around a lot. But hack couple of people to death with big knife? <u>NO WAY, O.J.!</u>
- As golfer, hate to "slice" (ha ha)

ITO, ITO, NOT SO NEATO
ITO, ITO, BAG OF FRITOS
HIROSHIMA, NUKE JUDGE ITO
BANZAI, BANZAI, NAGASAKI,
USE HIS HEAD FOR BACKYARD
HOCKEY!

GREAT IDEA! - BIG $$
SELL 100% GENUINE SAMPLES OF
O.J.'s DNA! NOT REAL STUFF - BLOOD
FROM RATS OR CHICKENS OR
SOMETHING

NOTE: Put Colin Ferguson on dream team?

WHY MY BLOOD WAS ALL OVER THE PLACE

- Always carry a razor - shave wherever I go (clean-cut image <u>very</u> important)
- Monster mosquitoes splatted on fence (distinctly remember loud buzzing sound)
- Popped huge zit, goo flew across yard.

ROSES ARE RED, VIOLETS ARE BLUE,
JUROR #66, I WANT TO BE
SEQUESTERED WITH YOU!

32 + 66

MONSTER BRONCO!

POLICE

JOHNNIE- NEED MORE
MYSTERY ENVELOPES

- A THIRD BLOODY GLOVE
- PHOTO OF ME AT HOME
  HOLDING BIG CLOCK ↘

MOM

- SAMPLE OF REAL KILLER'S
  DNA (ACTUALLY KETCHUP - HA HA)
- MAGIC ENDLESS HANDKERCHIEF
  (KEEP PULLING & PULLING &
  PULLING - GREAT GAG!
  JURY WILL LOVE IT!!)

JOHNNIE - POSSIB. ALIBI:
LONG LOST EVIL TWIN BROTHER (B.L.T. SIMPSON)
DID IT! - SEPARATED AT BIRTH BUT EXACTLY
THE SAME BLOOD TYPE, GLOVE PREFERENCE,
SHOE SIZE AND DNA!

⟶ WHAT I WAS DOING OUTSIDE THAT NIGHT ⟵

STUFF	PROBLEM
PRUNING HEDGES?	KATO'S JOB
WASHING CAR?	WHY CAR "DIRTY" ???
TAKING A LEAK?	TOO QUICK
MOWING LAWN?	SOMEONE WOULD HEAR IT
LOOKING FOR 4-LEAF CLOVER?	WHY NEED LUCK?!!!!!
DIGGING FOR WORMS?	DON'T FISH
PRACTICING GOLF SWING?	- BINGO! -

IDEAL JURY (MY PEERS)

JURY BOX ↑ THIS SIDE UP

HARD BOOK

U.S. MAIL

HARVARD LAW

I CONFESS!

NOT SO NICE THINGS I'VE DONE

① Endorsed Hertz but actually rented from Alamo.

② Improved lie, kicked ball out of sand trap, said "I had a six", etc.

③ Disregarded packaging instructions—"OPEN FROM OTHER END"—several occasions

④ Emptied Bentley's ashtrays onto street—cul de sac—Brentwood

⑤ On option play, intentionally grounded pass (never caught)

⑥ Took extra soap from maid's cart—Sonesta Hotel—Tahoe

⑦ Did ＊1 in Bob Evans' pool.

JOHNNIE-NEED MORE SYMPATHETIC JUDGE

• Judge Wapner
• Sammy Davis Jr. (might be dead)
• Clarence Thomas
• Flip Wilson

JOHNNIE-DO NOT LOVE JURY!

NEED ONE SLAM-DUNK JUROR TO DEADLOCK THIS SUCKER!

• GUY IN CIRCUS WHO THROWS KNIVES AT LADY?

• PROFESSIONAL BUTCHER OR UNION MEAT CUTTER? (SHOULD BE BIG FOOTBALL FAN, TOO)

• SUSHI CHEF?

• RODNEY KING! (WHO DO WE PAY AND HOW MUCH?)

POSSIB. ALIBI: WENT THROUGH OUT-OF-BODY EXPERIENCE— Spooky voices— swirly, lava-lamp type visions, intense feelings of INNOCENCE. Woke up at home in yard practicing golf swing with strange sense of loss etc. (read Shirley MacLaine on subj.?)

IMPORTANT! USE TIME IN JAIL CONSTRUCTIVELY!

✓ READ ENTIRE SET OF CLASSIC COMICS

✓ SUBSCRIBE TO INTELLECT. MAGS. (SPORTS ILLUS., PEOPLE, VANITY FAIR, ETC.)

✓ MEMORIZE MR. BOSTON BARTENDER GUIDE

✓ LEARN VENTRILOQUISM!

THROW VOICE AROUND COURTROOM

(JURY WILL LOVE IT!)

I DID IT!

NO, I DID IT!

CLASSIC COMICS! Billy Budd

JOHNNIE: POSSIB. REAL KILLER: THIRD MENENDEZ BROTHER!!! (LANCE MENENDEZ— HA HA)

DENISE ON STAND TODAY - <u>ACT PISSED</u> !

- Give her dirty looks?
- Make fart sounds to distract jury?

BOB. SHAP. - JUST A THOUGHT-
RUN LIKE HELL FOR DOOR?
NO!

LIGHTEN UP, ROBERTO!
JUST KIDDING!!! NOTE FOR FUTURE: BOB. SHAP.
HAS <u>**NO**</u> SENSE OF HUMOR

FAYE
RESNICK
MAKEOVER
DOLL

PERFUME 0000

HOW I GOT CUT ON FINGER

- Punched out drug dealer hanging around Nicole's place

- Paper cut from Filofax diary page (the missing one that proves my innocence)

- Scraped knuckle on nutmeg grater during major spice rack reorganization (Got totally carried away - lost all sense of time)

- Cut? What cut? It's an old birthmark. (Have no idea why it suddenly started bleeding - <u>VERY</u> <u>CONCERNED</u> - might be finger cancer)

CALL RON SHIPP - TELL HIM ALL FORGIVEN-
GET HIM TO PICK UP LAUNDRY, CHECK HOUSE
FOR LEAKS AFTER BIG RAIN,
MOW LAWN

I DIDN'T DO IT. I DIDN'T DO IT.
I DOODN'T DID IT. I DEEDN'T DO IT.
I DODN'T DEED IT.
THAT'S THE TRUTH, FOLKS!

PEOPLE WHO HAVE DONE A LOT WORSE THINGS THAN ME

- Hitler
- Dahmer
- Oliver Stone
- Headwaiter at Spago

✳ MAKE PRISON EXERCISE VIDEO?

PROBLEM: DOWNSCALE MARKET: CONS, LOSERS, ETC.

✳✳ BETTER IDEA— **O.J. SINGS THE BLUES** (LIP SYNC)

SELL ON QVC— O.J. LIVE FROM JAIL

✳✳✳ EVEN BETTER IDEA— *MAKE RAP VIDEO*

My name is O.J. and I'm here to say
I never went to Bundy on that Sunday
The truth and nothing but is all I want to tell
So why did you go and throw me in a cell.
Well, I can live without my Bentley and my microwave
My Rolex and my golf clubs and my—

F.LEE B.— WHAT RHYMES WITH "MICROWAVE"?

LL COOL O.J.?

O.J. HAMMER?

LASER GAV

O.J.?

 **LOOK!**

POSSIBLE NEW THEORY: L.A. RAMS DID IT
THAT'S WHY THEY HAD TO BEAT IT OUT OF TOWN!

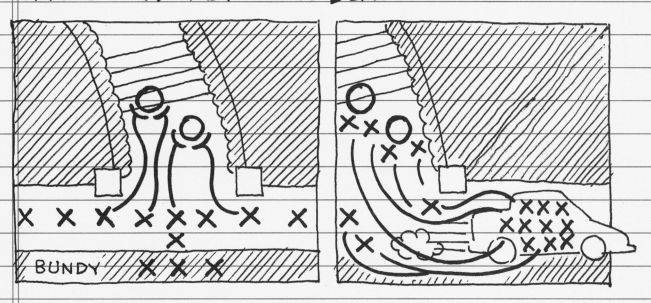

BUNDY

NOTE — POSSIB. TRIAL-OF-THE-CENTURY SOUVENIRS

- O.J., JOHNNIE C., BOB. SHAP. ACTION FIGURES (COLLECT THEM ALL!)  J.C.

- ACTUAL TIES WORN BY THE <u>DREAM TEAM</u> AND <u>YRS. TRULY</u> IN COURT (MAKE 1000'S OF THEM — WHO'S COUNTING?)

- SIGNED & FRAMED COURTROOM DRAWINGS (HOUSE LAYOUT, ETC.) LIMITED EDITION (1,000,000)

B. SHAP. TIE → $ $ $ $

 TRIAL ... CENTURY

- TRIAL OF THE CENTURY T-SHIRTS, CAPS, MUGS, LETTER OPENERS, MINIATURE GAVELS ETC. (MIGHT BE TOO TACKY?)

 IAL ... TURY

AL COWLINGS HAS 900# ???
BETTER GET GOING ON MY OWN 900 NUMBERS!

- I WANT TO TELL YOU — ON THE PHONE? PROMISE REAL INSIDE STUFF

- MARITAL ADVICE? (NAH)

- O.J.'S HOROSCOPE TIPS? (LOOK OUT FOR DARK, HANDSOME MEN! HAHA)

- O.J.'S TIME AND WEATHER? (WHAT THE HELL, GIVE IT A SHOT!)

POSSIB. COMMERCIAL ENDORSEMENTS
FOR AFTER I GET OFF

- RENT-A-WRECK (HUMBLE ANGLE)
- GINSU KNIFE (bad taste?)
- CELLULAR PHONES (CELL PHONES! - HA HA)

BOOK SEQUEL TITLES

TRY OUT ON JOHNNIE, BOB. SHAP. AND F. LEE B. (FLEEB!)

- WOULD YOU BELIEVE?
- WHAT'S YOUR POINT?
- WOULD I LIE TO YOU?
- BUT SERIOUSLY, FOLKS
- I WANT TO TELL YOU THE ABSOLUTELY ONE MILLION PERCENT TOTAL TRUTH

✳ OTHER BIG BOOK IDEAS-

- Tell-all book (tell-some? tell-none?) great first line, "Call me Orenthal..."
- Where's Waldo type book- Have to find O.J. in really complicated drawings...
- Drippy from-the-heart poetry book- "I know why caged dude sings blues" (Ask Larry S. if he can do rhyming stuff- possib. tie-in with prison video)
- Trial-of-Century crossword puzzle book

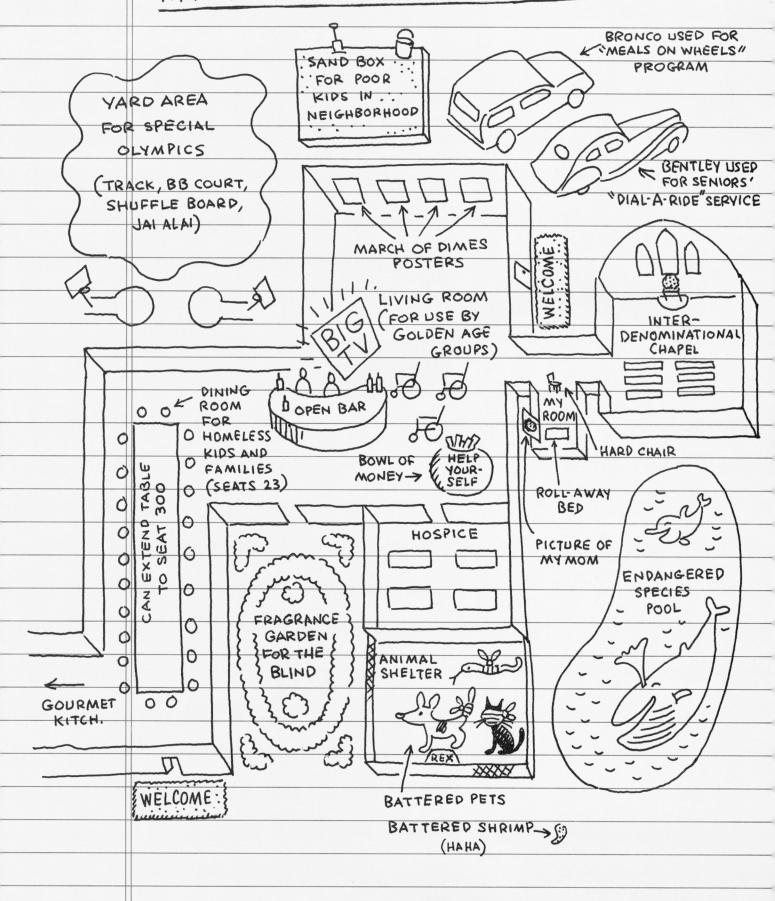

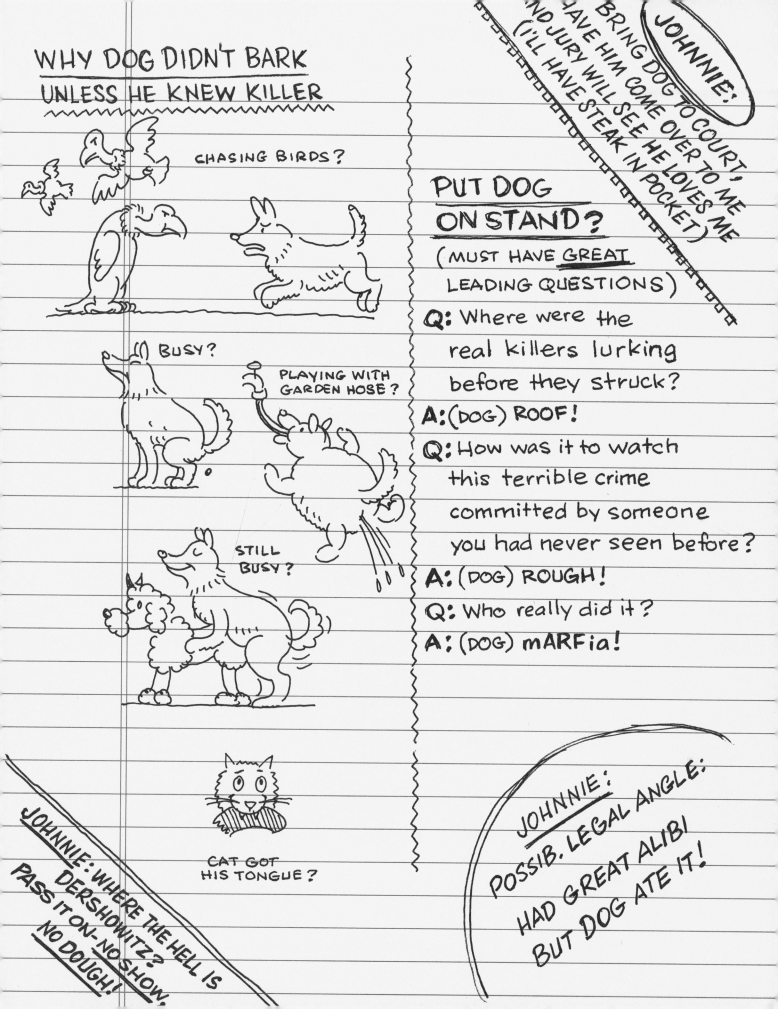

JOHNNIE—
DON'T KNOW ABOUT ROSA—
SEEMS A COUPLE OF TACOS SHY
OF A COMBINATION PLATE

BOB. SHA:.
MAKE SURE RO:
KNOWS I REALLY
DIG SPANISH
CHICKS!

JOHNNIE— WE'RE SUNK WITH ROSA
ON THIS TIME THING. MIGHT AS WELL HAD HER
SAY "SAW BRONCO BLANCO AT 2 HAIRS PAST A
FRECKLE EASTERN ELBOW TIME"!

ROSA'S CLOCK →

OKAY GUYS, ROSA WAS A GREAT GAG,
BUT SERIOUSLY, WHEN DO WE GET TO A
WITNESS WHO DOESN'T WEAR A
VELOUR JUMPSUIT?

JOHNNIE: OUR EXHIBITS SUCK!
NEED BETTER STUFF!

ACCORDION (COULD'VE MADE "PLAINTIVE WAIL" SOUND
AT BUNDY)

← METEORITE (DITTO, ALSO THUMPS ON KATO'S WALL)

← MALTESE PIGEON?

← CHIMPANZEE (PLAYED ACCORDION, MAYBE DID OTHER
"MONKEY BUSINESS" – SOW SEEDS OF DOUBT)

← VACUUM CLEANER PARTS (DID BERSERK DOOR-TO-DOOR
SALESMAN DO IT? JURY'S GOT TO WONDER!)

← FINGERPRINT FOUND AT CRIME SCENE

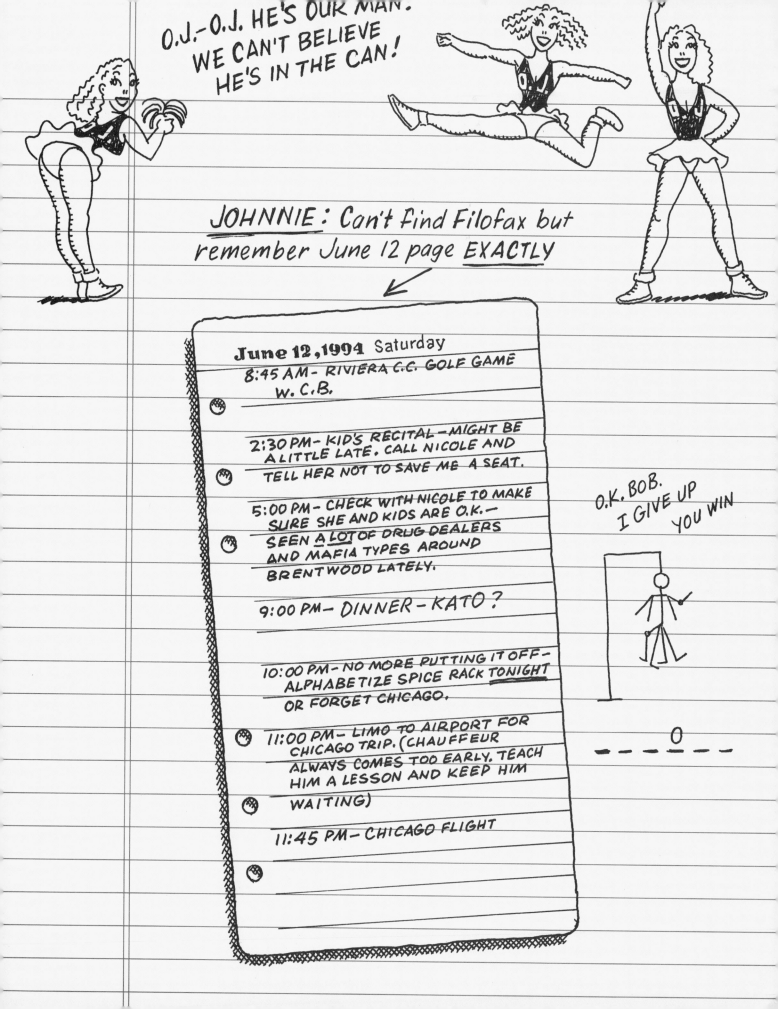

GUYS!
I'M TIRED OF PRESS
COVERAGE OF HASSLE
BETWEEN BOB. SHAP AND F. LEE B.
GODDAMIT, WHOSE TRIAL IS
THIS ANYWAY !!!!

THE
FLEEB →

F. LEE B. → NEED ONE MORE MARINE-TO-MARINE CONVERSATION WITH CORDOVA

"How would you like to earn ten thousand bucks in a real hurry?"

HOW FUHRMAN HID GLOVE
- STUCK GLOVE IN FLY AND ZIPPED IT UP (PLENTY OF ROOM)
- HAD BASEBALL— SAID HE WAS BREAKING IN GLOVE
- PAINTED EYES AND MOUTH ON GLOVE — MADE CUTE HAND PUPPET   HI KIDS!
- WORE IT AS SOCK

OTHER FAMOUS GUYS WHO BEAT RAP

GUY	PROB
Claus Von Bureau	Weird technicality
Guy who shot Liberty Valance	Just a movie
Guy who really shot JFK	Got off scot free but couldn't cash in
Mafia goombahs	End up dead
Network exec who axed Star Trek	Dumb, but not crime

LIAR LIAR
PANTS ON FIRE !

BOB. SHAP.-
O.K. IF I TEAR THIS
OFF AND PASS IT TO DARDEN?

NO

WHAT KATO AND I HAD AT McDONALD'S THAT NIGHT

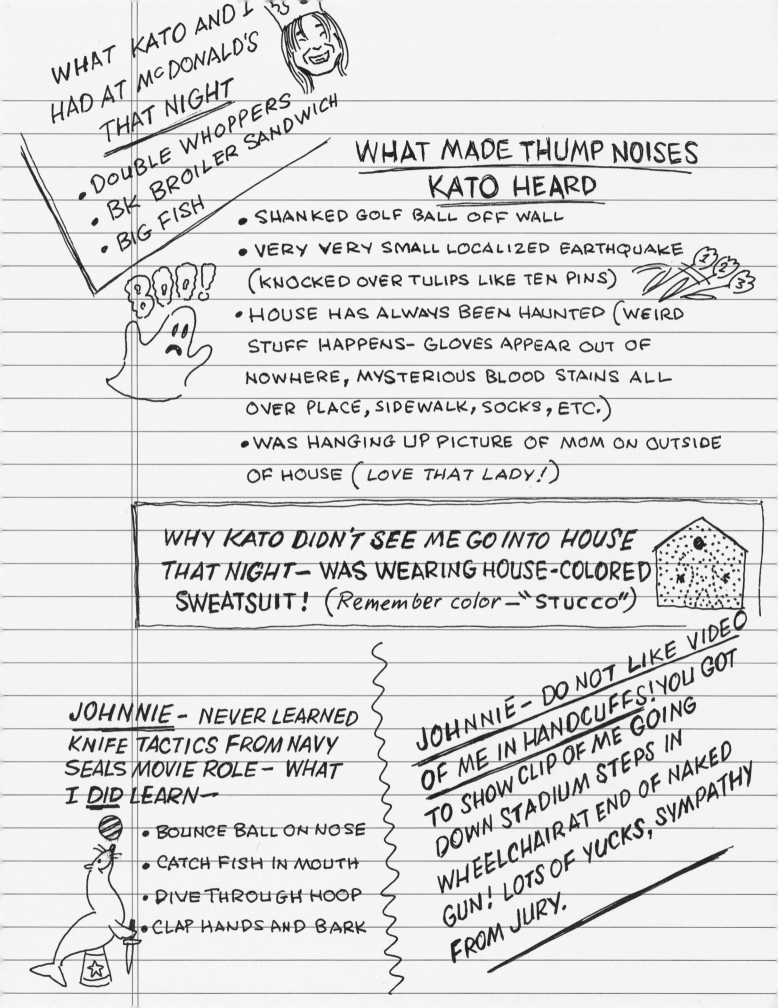

- DOUBLE WHOPPERS
- BK BROILER SANDWICH
- BIG FISH

BOO!

WHAT MADE THUMP NOISES KATO HEARD

- SHANKED GOLF BALL OFF WALL
- VERY VERY SMALL LOCALIZED EARTHQUAKE (KNOCKED OVER TULIPS LIKE TEN PINS)
- HOUSE HAS ALWAYS BEEN HAUNTED (WEIRD STUFF HAPPENS- GLOVES APPEAR OUT OF NOWHERE, MYSTERIOUS BLOOD STAINS ALL OVER PLACE, SIDEWALK, SOCKS, ETC.)
- WAS HANGING UP PICTURE OF MOM ON OUTSIDE OF HOUSE (LOVE THAT LADY!)

WHY *KATO DIDN'T SEE ME GO INTO HOUSE THAT NIGHT*- WAS WEARING HOUSE-COLORED SWEATSUIT! (Remember color - "STUCCO")

JOHNNIE- NEVER LEARNED KNIFE TACTICS FROM NAVY SEALS MOVIE ROLE - WHAT I DID LEARN→

- BOUNCE BALL ON NOSE
- CATCH FISH IN MOUTH
- DIVE THROUGH HOOP
- CLAP HANDS AND BARK

JOHNNIE- DO NOT LIKE VIDEO OF ME IN HANDCUFFS! YOU GOT TO SHOW CLIP OF ME GOING DOWN STADIUM STEPS IN WHEELCHAIR AT END OF NAKED GUN! LOTS OF YUCKS, SYMPATHY FROM JURY.

BORING BORING BORING Bo-Ring

GUYS! CAN'T WE SPEED THIS THING UP ?!!!!
OR DO I HAVE TO FIND SOME REAL FUN THINGS TO DO?

- DRY HEAVING
- HAVING ROOT CANAL
- BACK IN HIGH SCHOOL MATH CLASS
- LISTENING TO ZUCKERS EXPLAIN THEORY
  OF MOVIE COMEDY

JOHNNIE: What the hell is **DNA** anyway?
Can't we get some quack to say I have
BNA or **CDNA** or **LSMFTNA**, so it couldn't
possibly have been me?

JOHNNIE: WHAT'S AN 8-LETTER WORD THAT
MEANS "FALL DOWN"? SECOND LETTER MIGHT BE "L"

Plummet?

NOT ENOUGH LETTERS. HOW ABOUT "RIVER IN
EGYPT", 4 LETTERS, THIRD IS DEFINITELY "L"

BILL?

A RIVER NAMED BILL?!!
COME ON GUYS!
YOU'RE NOT TRYING!

KAMIKAZE

U.S.S. SIMPSON

MOM

O.J. O.K.

(BOB.SHAP.)

NEED LOTS OF CHARACTER WITNESSES

- 8TH grade math teacher, Miss Entwistle (HAD HOTS FOR ME)
- guy who makes cappuccino at Molto Latte (ALWAYS TIPPED BIG — NOW IT'S PAYBACK!)
- valet parker at Ivy (FAT KID WITH LISP — **LOVED** ME IN NAKED GUN)
- Advt. Dir. at Hertz (HIS ASS ON LINE BIG TIME!)
- caddies at golf club (Mr. Simpson? — always plays by rules, never loses temper, *blah-blah-blah*)
- Gerald Ford (HELPED HIM WITH SWING AT HOPE CLASSIC)
- Bob Shapiro (SURE HE'S MY LAWYER, BUT THE GUY IS PURE GOLD — HE'LL SAY **ANYTHING**!

Hurtz

JOHNNIE: IF I TESTIFY I WANT MY **OWN** TELESTRATOR OR AT LEAST ONE OF THOSE ROSS PEROT POINTERS

O.	O.	O.				
	O.					
O.	O.	O.	O.	O.	O.	O.
	J.	J.	J.	J.	J.	
J.	J.	J.			J.	
		J.	J.			

"THE PROF"

DESPERATELY NEED NEW WITNESSES FOR DEFENSE

- ☒ Joe Isuzu
- ☒ Crazy Eddie ➤➤
- ☒ Ivan Boesky
- ☒ Guy Colin Ferguson was going to call who said CIA put chip in his brain to make him robot assassin
- ☒ Hand out fliers in East L.A. — come on stand, mucho dinero!

WHAT I MIGHT BE WILLING TO PLEAD
SORT OF GUILTY TO

— Accessory to going too slow in fast lane of San Diego Freeway (ck with AL)

— Felony littering—blood, gloves, knit cap, etc. (Big fine, <u>no jail time</u>)

— Aggravated reckless conspiracy to loiter with intent to allegedly disturb the peace in the third degree.

— Leaving the scene of a potential made-for-TV movie.

FIRE LAWYERS—TAKE OVER DEFENSE LIKE C. FERGUSON?

◀ PROS ▶	◀ CONS ▶
① Aren't 43 witnesses in court who say I shot them	① If shit hits fan can't fire lawyers
② Save about 5 million bucks	② Don't know when to object to stuff
③ Lots of TV exposure—career plus	③ Might lose temper, slap Marcia Clark around
④ Look great in suits	④ Basically clueless

✳ EXTENUATING CIRCUMSTANCES

• GOING PREMATURELY BALD—MIDLIFE CRISIS <u>BIGTIME</u>

• NAME BRUTALLY SHORTENED WHEN I WAS KID— ALL MY LIFE CALLED BY MY INITIALS — HUMILIATED

• BLACK RAGE (TALK TO KUNSTLER— IF WON'T WASH, TRY BLACK ANNOYANCE? BLACK PEEVISHNESS?)

• DEVIL MADE ME DO IT!! (HA HA)

JOHNNIE—TELL LARRY SCHILLER— JUST RECEIVED GREAT LETTER FOR SEQUEL!

DEAR O.J.—

I SAW ~~EVERYTHING~~ THE WHOLE THING — ~~A COUPLE OF GUYS~~ SIX GUYS IN ~~SKI MASKS~~ CAMOUFLAGE FATIGUES CARRYING ~~BIG GUNS~~ COMMANDO KNIVES JUMPED OUT OF A ~~HELICOPTER~~ MINIVAN WITH COLOMBIAN LICENSE PLATES PARKED IN THE ALLEY OFF BUNDY. THEY WERE CARRYING A BOX MARKED PUPPY SNOOZE MIX, WHICH I GUESS EXPLAINS WHY THE DOG DIDN'T BARK. I THINK THEY SAW ME — THAT'S WHY I DON'T DARE COME FORWARD. I SURE HOPE THIS NOTE I WROTE ON A PIECE OF YELLOW LEGAL PAPER HELPS YOUR CASE.

A FRIEND

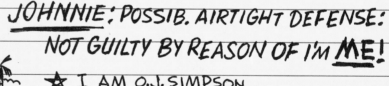

JOHNNIE: POSSIB. AIRTIGHT DEFENSE: NOT GUILTY BY REASON OF I'M ME!

★ I AM O.J. SIMPSON

★ O.J. SIMPSON COULDN'T POSSIBLY HAVE DONE IT

★ THEREFORE: NO WAY O.J.!

NOTE: What about Michael Jackson? How come no one asks him about his other glove?

IF PAULA COMES TO COURT, MUST WEAR (GIVE HER SOME CHOICES):

- NUN'S HABIT
- AMISH OUTFIT (OVERALLS, STRAW HAT, BEARD)
- SPACE SUIT
- MR. PEANUT COSTUME

MEZZALUNA
TAKE-OUT

Phone # ?

LINE OF
LUGGAGE?

ACTING PARTS FOR KATO –
TYPE CASTING!

- Non-paying houseguest in Dr. Quinn, Medicine Woman
- Deadbeat Brady in Brady Bunch sequel - lives in closet
- Freeloading space alien in new Star Trek

JOHNNIE: GREAT IDEA, BUT IF YOU DO IT, I GET A PIECE

THE TONIGHT SHOW STARRING JOHNNIE COCHRAN!

Celeb guests but they're all under oath! You ask really embarrassing questions, and they have to tell truth or go to jail.

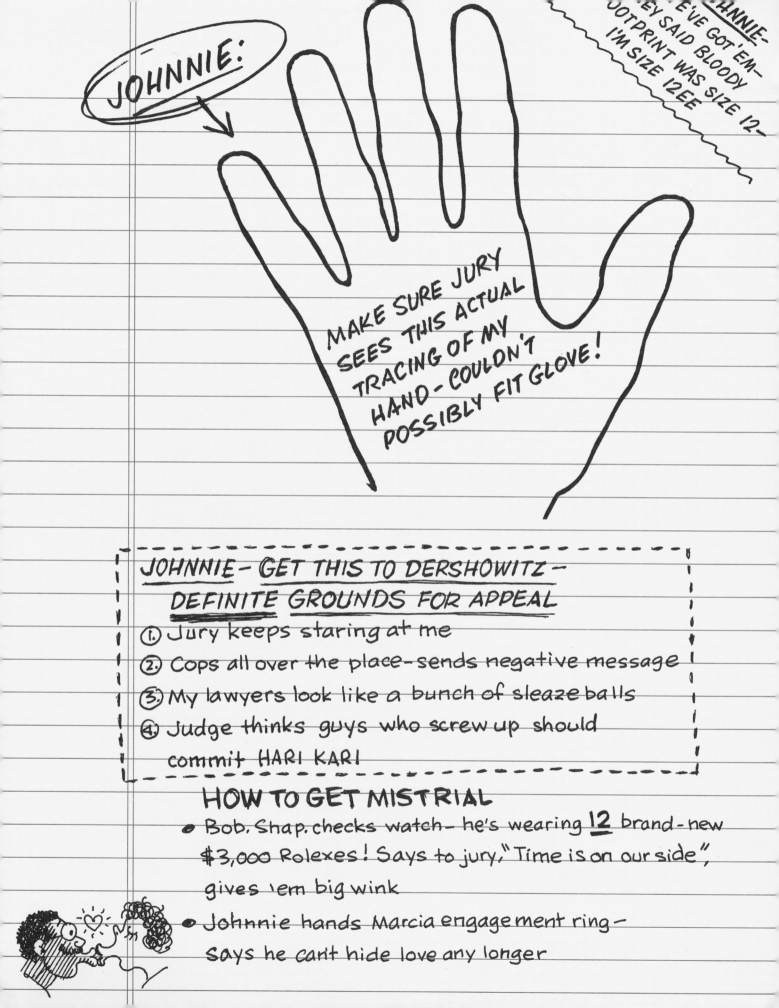

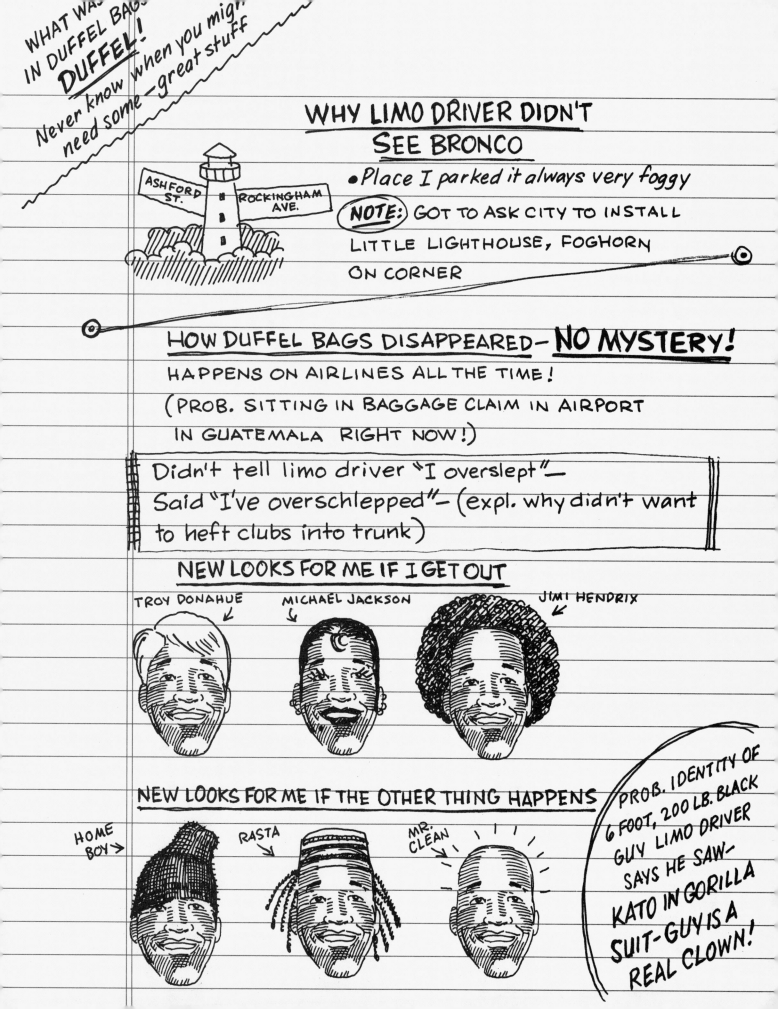

JOHNNIE: GREAT STUFF FOR CLOSING ARGUMENT

- QUOTES FROM BIBLE WHERE GOD TELLS GUYS TO ICE WIVES WHO FORNICATE, COMMIT ADULTERY
- DITTO — PILLAR OF SALT, SAMSON & DELILAH
    O.J. SAMPSON! →
- LOCKER-ROOM-STYLE PEP TALK — GO IN THERE AND WIN ONE FOR OLD #32
- HAND OUT $100 BILLS

AI-YEEE!

BLAH BLAH BLAH

IF I GO DOWN, I'M TAKING THEM WITH ME

- BARNEY
- MICKEY
- FLIPPER
- KERMIT
- LASSIE
- LAMBCHOP
- GUMBY

8693251   8693251

BIG BUCKS BOOK IDEA
Sell rights to O.J.'s legal pad
(Don't tell those killjoys Johnnie and Bob. Shap.)

NOTE — NEED TO FIND REALLY SLEAZY PUBLISHER

Thanks to
Ward Calhoun, Carol Boswell, David Rosenthal, Gwyneth Cravens, Chris "Milk-Through-
the-Nose" Allison, Annik LaFarge, Leta Evanthes, Andy and Susan Borowitz, Mac Davis,
Patty Brown, Tad Floridis, Dan Rembert, Adam Rothberg, and Roger Bilheimer.